THE MINDFUL ENTREPRENEUR: CULTIVATING SUCCESS WITH PRESENCE AND PURPOSE

BY

TONY D.

Table of Contents

Introduction:

In today's fast-paced, ever-evolving world, the entrepreneurial landscape

has become a fascinating amalgamation of innovation, risk-taking, and

opportunity. Entrepreneurs are the driving force behind groundbreaking ideas, disruptive technologies, and new business ventures that shape our society. They possess a unique ability to identify gaps in the market, envision possibilities, and transform their dreams into reality. However, the path of entrepreneurship is not without its challenges.

Building a successful business requires more than just a brilliant idea or a strategic plan. It demands resilience, adaptability, and a deep understanding of oneself and the surrounding environment. In the quest for success, entrepreneurs often find themselves grappling with stress, burnout, and a constant battle to maintain work-life balance. The pressure to compete, make tough decisions, and keep up with the ever-changing market dynamics can take a toll on their well-being.

It is in this complex and demanding entrepreneurial landscape that the concept of mindfulness emerges as a powerful tool for success and personal growth. Mindfulness, rooted in ancient contemplative practices, has gained widespread recognition in recent years for its ability to enhance focus, clarity, and emotional intelligence. By cultivating a mindful mindset, entrepreneurs can navigate the challenges of entrepreneurship with presence and purpose, leading to not only professional success but also a sense of fulfillment and well-being.

"The Mindful Entrepreneur: Cultivating Success with Presence and Purpose" is a guidebook that explores the intersection of mindfulness and entrepreneurship, delving into the transformative potential of integrating mindfulness practices into the entrepreneurial journey. This book aims to provide entrepreneurs, aspiring business owners, and anyone interested in mindful living with practical strategies, inspiring stories, and thought-provoking insights to cultivate success in business and in life.

Chapter 1: The Entrepreneur's Journey

To embark on the path of mindful entrepreneurship, it is crucial to understand the evolution of entrepreneurship and its significance in today's world. This chapter sets the stage by tracing the roots of entrepreneurship and examining its transformation in the digital age. We explore the qualities and skills that make a successful entrepreneur and the various roles they play, from innovator to leader to problem-solver. By gaining a holistic understanding of the entrepreneurial journey, we lay the foundation for the integration of mindfulness into this dynamic realm.

The chapter also highlights the role of mindfulness in entrepreneurship. Mindfulness, at its core, is about being fully present in the moment, with an open and non-judgmental awareness. It offers entrepreneurs the ability to focus their attention, make conscious decisions, and respond skillfully to challenges and opportunities. We delve into the science behind mindfulness, exploring the research that supports its benefits for mental well-being, creativity, and resilience. By understanding the neurological and psychological mechanisms of mindfulness, entrepreneurs can embrace it as a valuable tool for success.

Part I: Developing a Mindful Mindset

Chapter 2: The Power of Presence

In a world filled with distractions and information overload, the ability to be fully present becomes a superpower. This chapter dives deep into the concept of presence and its significance in the entrepreneurial journey. We explore mindfulness practices that cultivate present moment awareness, such as breath awareness, body scans, and sensory grounding. By integrating these practices into their daily lives, entrepreneurs can enhance their focus, reduce stress, and tap into their innate creativity.

The chapter also addresses the challenges that entrepreneurs often face when attempting to be present, such as multitasking, the fear of missing out (FOMO), and the relentless pursuit of productivity. We discuss strategies to overcome these challenges and create space for intentional presence, allowing entrepreneurs to make clear decisions, nurture meaningful relationships, and fully engage with their work.

Chapter 3: Aligning with Purpose

While entrepreneurs are often driven by a desire for financial success, true fulfillment comes from aligning their work with a higher purpose.

In this chapter, we explore the importance of discovering and embracing one's entrepreneurial purpose. We delve into the process of self-reflection, identifying personal values, and exploring the deeper meaning behind one's entrepreneurial aspirations. By aligning their work with their values and passions, entrepreneurs can create a sense of purpose that fuels their motivation, resilience, and long-term success.

We guide readers through exercises and self-inquiry practices to uncover their unique entrepreneurial purpose. We discuss the power of creating a vision and mission statement that serves as a compass, guiding entrepreneurs through the ups and downs of their journey. With a clear sense of purpose, entrepreneurs can find meaning in their work, attract like-minded collaborators, and build businesses that make a positive impact on the world.

Chapter 4: Embracing Uncertainty and Resilience

Entrepreneurship is synonymous with uncertainty. The ability to embrace and navigate uncertainty is a vital skill for any entrepreneur. In this chapter, we delve into the mindset and practices that cultivate resilience and adaptability in the face of challenges.

We explore the psychological and emotional aspects of uncertainty, discussing common fears and anxieties that entrepreneurs encounter. By cultivating mindfulness and self-compassion, entrepreneurs can build the resilience necessary to weather the storms of entrepreneurship. We provide practical tools and strategies to develop a growth mindset, reframe setbacks as learning opportunities, and maintain a sense of balance and equanimity amidst uncertainty.

Through personal anecdotes and case studies, we highlight the stories of resilient entrepreneurs who have faced adversity and emerged stronger. By learning from their experiences, readers can gain inspiration and insights into how to overcome obstacles and thrive in the face of uncertainty.

Part I of "The Mindful Entrepreneur: Cultivating Success with Presence and Purpose" lays the groundwork for developing a mindful mindset. By understanding the entrepreneurial journey, embracing presence, aligning with purpose, and cultivating resilience, entrepreneurs are better equipped to navigate the challenges and uncertainties they will encounter. In Part II, we delve into specific mindful strategies that entrepreneurs can employ to enhance their decision-making, leadership, communication, and work environment.

Chapter 1: The Entrepreneur's Journey

Introduction:

Entrepreneurship is not merely a career choice; it is a transformative journey that demands vision, passion, and an unwavering commitment to bring about change. In this chapter, we embark on an exploration of the evolution of entrepreneurship, the diverse roles that entrepreneurs play, and the significance of their contributions in shaping the world we live in today. By understanding the essence of the entrepreneurial journey, we lay the foundation for integrating mindfulness into this dynamic realm.

The Evolution of Entrepreneurship:

Entrepreneurship has existed in various forms throughout history. From the ancient traders who embarked on perilous voyages to explore new markets to the modern-day innovators who disrupt industries with groundbreaking technologies, entrepreneurs have always played a crucial role in driving economic growth and societal progress.

In this section, we trace the evolution of entrepreneurship, from its earliest roots to the present day. We explore how entrepreneurship has evolved alongside changes in technology, culture, and economic systems. We examine the rise of the industrial revolution and the emergence of the knowledge economy, which have provided new opportunities and challenges for entrepreneurs.

The Changing Roles of Entrepreneurs:

Entrepreneurs are not confined to a single role or responsibility. They wear many hats, adapting and evolving as their ventures grow. In this section, we delve into the diverse roles that entrepreneurs play throughout their journey:

1. **The Visionary:** Entrepreneurs possess a unique ability to see opportunities where others see obstacles. They have a vision of a better future and the determination to turn that vision into reality. We explore how entrepreneurs cultivate and communicate their vision, inspiring others to join them on their entrepreneurial journey.

2. **The Innovator:** Entrepreneurship is driven by innovation. Entrepreneurs challenge the status quo, disrupt industries, and bring forth new solutions to address unmet needs. We discuss the mindset and creative processes that enable entrepreneurs to innovate and remain at the forefront of their fields.

3. **The Leader:** As their ventures grow, entrepreneurs assume leadership roles. We explore the qualities and skills that make an effective

entrepreneurial leader, such as strategic thinking, adaptability, and the ability to inspire and motivate others. We delve into the importance of cultivating authentic leadership, based on integrity, empathy, and a genuine connection with one's team.

4. The Risk-Taker: Entrepreneurship inherently involves risk-taking. Entrepreneurs embrace uncertainty, make bold decisions, and are willing to venture into uncharted territories. We examine the mindset and strategies that enable entrepreneurs to manage risk effectively and navigate the challenges that arise along the way.

5. The Problem-Solver: Entrepreneurs are driven by a desire to solve problems and meet unmet needs. They identify gaps in the market, develop innovative solutions, and create value for their customers. We discuss the problem-solving mindset and approaches that entrepreneurs employ to address complex challenges.

6. The Networker: Building a strong network is crucial for entrepreneurial success. Entrepreneurs thrive by forging connections, collaborating with others, and accessing valuable resources. We explore the importance of networking and provide practical tips for entrepreneurs to build and nurture meaningful relationships within their industries.

The Significance of Entrepreneurship in Today's World:

Entrepreneurship has become an integral part of our global economy and society. In this section, we examine the significance of entrepreneurship in addressing societal challenges, driving economic growth, and fostering innovation. We discuss how entrepreneurship contributes to job creation, wealth generation, and the development of sustainable solutions.

Furthermore, entrepreneurship is not limited to traditional business ventures. Social entrepreneurship has emerged as a powerful force for positive change, combining business principles with a social or environmental mission. We explore the impact of social entrepreneurship and its potential to address pressing global issues.

The chapter concludes by emphasizing the importance of mindfulness in the context of entrepreneurship. Mindfulness offers entrepreneurs the

tools to navigate the challenges, uncertainties, and fast-paced nature of their journey. By cultivating present moment awareness, entrepreneurs can make conscious decisions, foster creativity, and maintain their well-being amidst the demands of entrepreneurship.

Chapter 1 provides a comprehensive overview of the entrepreneurial journey, from its historical roots to its current significance in our modern world. By understanding the diverse roles of entrepreneurs and the evolving landscape in which they operate, readers gain a deeper appreciation for the challenges and opportunities that lie ahead. In the following chapters, we delve into the integration of mindfulness into the entrepreneurial journey, providing practical strategies and insights to cultivate success with presence and purpose.

Part I: Developing a Mindful Mindset

In Part I of "The Mindful Entrepreneur: Cultivating Success with Presence and Purpose," we lay the foundation for developing a mindful mindset. This section explores the essential elements that contribute to a mindful approach to entrepreneurship.

Through chapters focused on the power of presence, aligning with purpose, and embracing uncertainty and resilience, readers will gain valuable insights and practical strategies to cultivate a mindful mindset. By integrating mindfulness practices into their daily lives, entrepreneurs can enhance their focus, decision-making abilities, and overall well-being, setting the stage for success in their entrepreneurial journey.

Part I sets the stage for the subsequent sections of the book, where we delve into specific mindful strategies for entrepreneurial success and explore real-life stories of mindful entrepreneurs who have achieved remarkable accomplishments.

Chapter 2: The Power of Presence

Introduction:

In a world filled with distractions and constant stimulation, the ability to be fully present is a rare and valuable skill. Entrepreneurs who cultivate presence gain a competitive edge by sharpening their focus, enhancing decision-making abilities, and connecting more deeply with themselves and others. In this chapter, we delve into the concept of presence and its profound impact on the entrepreneurial journey. We explore mindfulness practices that cultivate present moment awareness and provide practical strategies for entrepreneurs to integrate presence into their daily lives.

Understanding Presence:

Presence, in its essence, refers to being fully engaged and aware in the present moment, without being swept away by thoughts of the past or worries about the future. It involves directing our attention to the here and now, fostering a deep connection with our experiences, thoughts, and emotions. When entrepreneurs cultivate presence, they become more attuned to their surroundings, allowing them to seize opportunities, respond effectively to challenges, and make informed decisions.

The Benefits of Presence:

Being present offers a multitude of benefits for entrepreneurs. Research has shown that cultivating presence through mindfulness practices improves cognitive functioning, enhances emotional intelligence, reduces stress, and increases overall well-being. By developing a mindful awareness of the present moment, entrepreneurs can experience the following benefits:

1. Enhanced Focus and Concentration: Presence enables entrepreneurs to channel their attention towards what truly matters, eliminating distractions and honing their focus on critical tasks. As a result, they become more efficient and productive, accomplishing more in less time.

2. Heightened Creativity and Innovation: Presence allows entrepreneurs to tap into their creative potential by quieting the mental chatter and opening themselves to fresh ideas and perspectives. In a state of presence, they can think outside the box, explore new possibilities, and develop innovative solutions.

3. Improved Decision-Making: By cultivating presence, entrepreneurs develop greater clarity and insight. They can make decisions with a clear and balanced mind, relying on their intuition and wisdom. Being fully present in the decision-making process helps entrepreneurs avoid impulsive choices and consider a wider range of possibilities.

4. Strengthened Relationships and Communication: Presence fosters better interpersonal connections by allowing entrepreneurs to listen attentively, empathize genuinely, and engage in meaningful conversations. Being fully present in interactions enables entrepreneurs to build trust, understand others' perspectives, and form deeper connections with team members, clients, and partners.

Cultivating Presence through Mindfulness:

Mindfulness, the practice of paying deliberate attention to the present moment, is a powerful tool for cultivating presence. In this section, we explore mindfulness practices that entrepreneurs can incorporate into their daily lives:

1. Breath Awareness: The breath serves as an anchor to the present moment. By bringing attention to the breath, entrepreneurs can ground themselves in the here and now, fostering a sense of calm and clarity. We guide readers through breath awareness exercises and offer tips for integrating mindful breathing into their entrepreneurial routine.

2. Body Scans: Body scans involve systematically directing awareness through different parts of the body, observing physical sensations without judgment. This practice enhances body-mind connection and helps entrepreneurs become more attuned to subtle signals of stress or tension. We provide step-by-step instructions for body scan exercises.

3. Sensory Awareness: Sensory awareness involves intentionally engaging with our senses to cultivate present moment awareness. By immersing ourselves in the sensory experiences of sight, sound, touch, taste, and smell, entrepreneurs can anchor themselves in the present moment and fully appreciate their surroundings.

Overcoming Challenges to Presence:

Entrepreneurs face numerous challenges that can hinder their ability to be present. Distractions, multitasking, and the pressure to constantly be connected can fragment attention and drain mental energy. In this section, we address common challenges to presence and provide strategies to overcome them:

1. Digital Detox: We discuss the importance of periodically disconnecting from digital devices and creating boundaries to protect time for presence and rejuvenation.

2. Mindful Time Management: Effective time management strategies, such as prioritizing tasks, setting realistic goals, and practicing single-tasking, enable entrepreneurs to focus their attention and create dedicated space for presence.

3. Cultivating Mindful Habits: We explore how incorporating simple mindfulness practices into daily routines, such as mindful eating, walking, or pausing for a moment of reflection, can strengthen the habit of presence.

Real-Life Examples of Presence in Action:

To bring the concept of presence to life, we share inspiring stories of successful entrepreneurs who embody presence in their work and lives.

These entrepreneurs demonstrate the transformative power of presence in overcoming challenges, fostering innovation, and cultivating thriving businesses.

Conclusion:

Chapter 2 highlights the immense power of presence for entrepreneurs. By cultivating presence through mindfulness practices and overcoming common challenges, entrepreneurs can sharpen their focus, tap into their creativity, make informed decisions, and build meaningful connections. Embracing the power of presence sets the stage for success and fulfillment on the entrepreneurial journey. In the next chapter, we explore the importance of aligning with purpose, delving into how entrepreneurs can find deeper meaning and create a sense of purpose that guides their entrepreneurial endeavors.

Chapter 3: Aligning with Purpose

Introduction:

Entrepreneurship without purpose is like sailing without a compass. Aligning with purpose is essential for entrepreneurs to find meaning in their work, fuel their motivation, and create a lasting impact. In this chapter, we delve into the profound significance of purpose in the entrepreneurial journey. We explore the process of self-reflection, identifying personal values, and uncovering the deeper meaning behind one's entrepreneurial aspirations. By aligning their work with purpose, entrepreneurs can cultivate a sense of fulfillment and guide their decisions and actions towards creating a meaningful and successful venture.

The Power of Purpose:

Purpose serves as a guiding light, a North Star that directs entrepreneurs towards their true calling. It provides a sense of direction, clarity, and motivation that transcends the pursuit of financial success. When entrepreneurs align their work with purpose, they tap into a deep well of passion, resilience, and commitment that fuels their journey.

In this section, we explore the significance of purpose in entrepreneurship. We discuss how purpose empowers entrepreneurs to overcome challenges, make bold decisions, and persevere in the face of adversity. We delve into research that highlights the correlation between purpose-driven businesses and long-term success, employee engagement, and customer loyalty. By understanding the power of purpose, entrepreneurs can embark on a transformative journey that transcends personal fulfillment and creates a positive impact on society.

Uncovering Personal Values and Passions:

To align with purpose, entrepreneurs must first delve inward and uncover their core values and passions. This process of self-reflection allows entrepreneurs to gain a deeper understanding of themselves and what truly matters to them. In this section, we guide readers through exercises and self-inquiry practices to explore their values, passions, and the unique gifts they bring to the world.

We discuss the importance of authenticity in aligning with purpose, encouraging entrepreneurs to embrace their true selves and build ventures that authentically reflect their values and passions. By understanding their personal values, entrepreneurs can make conscious decisions that are in alignment with their core beliefs, fostering a sense of integrity and coherence in their work.

Creating a Vision and Mission Statement:

Once entrepreneurs have identified their values and passions, they can create a vision and mission statement that encapsulates their purpose. A vision statement outlines the long-term aspirations and impact entrepreneurs seek to create, while a mission statement defines the purpose and values that guide their daily actions.

In this section, we provide practical guidance on crafting compelling vision and mission statements. We discuss the elements that make a vision and mission statement effective, such as clarity, inspiration, and alignment with personal values. By creating a powerful vision and mission statement, entrepreneurs can articulate their purpose to themselves, their team, and the world, setting a solid foundation for their entrepreneurial journey.

Integrating Purpose into Business Practices:

Aligning with purpose is not a one-time exercise; it requires ongoing commitment and integration into all aspects of entrepreneurship. In this section, we explore how entrepreneurs can infuse purpose into various business practices:

1. Product and Service Alignment: We discuss the importance of developing products or services that align with entrepreneurs' purpose and values. By creating offerings that address societal needs, entrepreneurs can build a customer base that resonates with their purpose and becomes advocates for their brand.

2. Stakeholder Engagement: Entrepreneurs can extend purpose alignment to their interactions with stakeholders, including employees, customers, suppliers, and communities. We explore the importance of fostering meaningful relationships, practicing ethical business conduct, and considering the broader societal impact of business decisions.

3. Social and Environmental Responsibility: Purpose-driven entrepreneurship goes beyond financial success; it encompasses a commitment to social and environmental responsibility. We discuss the integration of sustainability practices, corporate social responsibility initiatives, and conscious decision-making that prioritizes the well-being of people and the planet.

Real-Life Examples of Purpose-driven Entrepreneurs:

To illustrate the power of purpose in action, we share inspiring stories of purpose-driven entrepreneurs who have made a significant impact through their ventures. These entrepreneurs serve as role models, demonstrating how aligning with purpose can lead to remarkable success while creating positive change in the world.

Conclusion:

Chapter 3 emphasizes the transformative power of aligning with purpose in the entrepreneurial journey. By uncovering personal values, creating a vision and mission statement, and integrating purpose into business practices, entrepreneurs can cultivate a deep sense of fulfillment and guide their ventures towards meaningful impact. Aligning with purpose provides the foundation for a purpose-driven entrepreneurial journey that combines success with a lasting legacy. In the next chapter, we explore the importance of embracing uncertainty and resilience as entrepreneurs navigate the dynamic landscape of entrepreneurship.

Chapter 4: Embracing Uncertainty and Resilience

Introduction:

Entrepreneurship is inherently filled with uncertainty. The path of an entrepreneur is marked by unpredictable challenges, unforeseen obstacles, and constant change. In this chapter, we explore the importance of embracing uncertainty and cultivating resilience as essential qualities for entrepreneurial success. We delve into strategies for reframing uncertainty as an opportunity, developing resilience in the face of adversity, and maintaining mental and emotional well-being amidst the unpredictable nature of entrepreneurship.

The Nature of Uncertainty in Entrepreneurship:

Uncertainty is a fundamental aspect of the entrepreneurial journey. Market conditions, customer preferences, technological advancements, and economic fluctuations all contribute to an ever-shifting landscape. In this section, we discuss the nature of uncertainty in entrepreneurship, exploring the factors that contribute to it and the impact it has on entrepreneurs and their ventures.

We delve into the psychological and emotional challenges that uncertainty presents, including fear of failure, self-doubt, and decision paralysis. By understanding the dynamics of uncertainty, entrepreneurs can reframe their perspectives and develop strategies to navigate and thrive in unpredictable circumstances.

Reframing Uncertainty as an Opportunity:

While uncertainty can be daunting, it also presents an opportunity for growth and innovation. In this section, we explore strategies for reframing uncertainty as a catalyst for positive change:

1. Embracing the Growth Mindset: The growth mindset, characterized by a belief in the potential for growth and learning, allows entrepreneurs to view uncertainty as a stepping stone to progress. We discuss the principles of the growth mindset and provide practical tips for developing and nurturing it.

2. Embracing Failure: Failure is an inevitable part of the entrepreneurial journey. By embracing failure as a valuable learning experience, entrepreneurs can overcome the fear of failure and embrace experimentation, resilience, and adaptability. We explore how reframing failure as feedback fuels growth and innovation.

3. Cultivating Curiosity and Adaptability: Curiosity and adaptability are vital traits for navigating uncertainty. We discuss strategies for cultivating curiosity, such as asking open-ended questions, seeking diverse perspectives, and staying curious in the face of challenges. We also explore the importance of adaptability, including the ability to pivot, learn from setbacks, and adjust business strategies.

Developing Resilience in the Face of Adversity:

Resilience is the ability to bounce back from setbacks, adapt to change, and persevere in the face of challenges. In this section, we explore the importance of developing resilience as an entrepreneur:

1. Building a Strong Support Network: A supportive network of mentors, peers, and advisors plays a crucial role in fostering resilience. We discuss the importance of cultivating and nurturing relationships that provide emotional support, guidance, and constructive feedback.

2. Developing Emotional Intelligence: Emotional intelligence enables entrepreneurs to manage their emotions effectively, regulate stress, and navigate challenging situations with empathy and composure. We explore strategies for developing emotional intelligence, such as self-awareness, self-regulation, empathy, and effective communication.

3. Practicing Self-Care: The demanding nature of entrepreneurship can take a toll on mental and emotional well-being. We emphasize the importance of self-care and provide practical tips for entrepreneurs to prioritize their physical health, mental well-being, and work-life balance.

4. Embracing Mindfulness and Stress-Reduction Techniques: Mindfulness practices, such as meditation, deep breathing, and visualization, can help entrepreneurs cultivate resilience by calming the mind, enhancing focus, and reducing stress. We provide guidance on integrating mindfulness and stress-reduction techniques into the entrepreneurial routine.

Real-Life Examples of Resilient Entrepreneurs:

To inspire readers, we share real-life examples of resilient entrepreneurs who have faced significant challenges and setbacks but persevered to achieve success. These stories highlight the power of resilience in overcoming obstacles, adapting to change, and creating impactful ventures.

Conclusion:

Chapter 4 emphasizes the importance of embracing uncertainty and cultivating resilience as key qualities for entrepreneurial success. By reframing uncertainty as an opportunity, developing resilience in the face of adversity, and prioritizing mental and emotional well-being, entrepreneurs can navigate the unpredictable nature of entrepreneurship with confidence and determination. Embracing uncertainty and resilience empower entrepreneurs to thrive amidst challenges and propel their ventures towards long-term success. In the next chapter, we explore the concept of mindful decision-making and its significance in creating sustainable and impactful businesses.

Part II: Mindful Strategies for Entrepreneurial Success

In Part II of "The Mindful Entrepreneur: Cultivating Success with Presence and Purpose," we dive into mindful strategies that entrepreneurs can employ to enhance their success. This section explores specific areas of focus where mindfulness can make a profound impact on entrepreneurial endeavors.

From mindful leadership and effective communication to mindful innovation and strategic planning, Part II offers practical guidance and insights for entrepreneurs to integrate mindfulness into various aspects of their business. By applying mindful strategies, entrepreneurs can cultivate a harmonious balance between presence, purpose, and strategic action, leading to sustainable growth and meaningful impact.

Part II equips entrepreneurs with the tools and frameworks necessary to navigate the complex and dynamic entrepreneurial landscape with clarity, intention, and mindfulness. Through real-world examples and actionable steps, entrepreneurs will gain valuable insights and inspiration to infuse mindfulness into their daily practices and propel their ventures towards success.

Chapter 5: Mindful Decision Making

Introduction:

Decision-making is at the core of entrepreneurship, and the ability to make informed and effective choices is essential for success. However, the fast-paced and often chaotic nature of the entrepreneurial journey can make decision-making challenging. In this chapter, we explore the concept of mindful decision making and its profound impact on the entrepreneurial process. We delve into the principles of mindful decision making, provide practical techniques for cultivating a mindful approach, and highlight the benefits of integrating mindfulness into the decision-making process.

Understanding Mindful Decision Making:

Mindful decision making involves bringing conscious awareness to the decision-making process. It goes beyond analytical thinking and taps into intuition, emotional intelligence, and a deep understanding of the present moment. By cultivating mindfulness, entrepreneurs can make decisions that are aligned with their values, purpose, and long-term vision.

In this section, we explore the core principles of mindful decision making, including:

1. Presence and Awareness: Mindful decision making starts with being fully present and aware of the present moment. By observing thoughts, emotions, and external factors without judgment, entrepreneurs can gain clarity and make decisions from a place of centeredness.

2. Intuition and Gut Feelings: Mindfulness allows entrepreneurs to tap into their intuition and gut feelings, which often hold valuable insights that can guide decision making. We discuss techniques for accessing and trusting intuition as a valuable resource in the decision-making process.

3. Balancing Analytical and Intuitive Thinking: Mindful decision making combines analytical thinking with intuitive insights. We explore strategies for integrating rational analysis with intuitive wisdom, creating a balanced approach that considers both logical reasoning and intuitive guidance.

Cultivating Mindfulness for Decision Making:

To cultivate mindfulness in the decision-making process, entrepreneurs can practice specific techniques and develop daily habits. In this section, we explore mindfulness practices that enhance decision-making skills, including:

1. Mindful Observation: By bringing mindful awareness to the present moment, entrepreneurs can observe their thoughts, emotions, and bodily sensations related to the decision at hand. We discuss techniques such as mindful breathing and body scans to develop a heightened sense of awareness.

2. Reflective Inquiry: Reflective inquiry involves asking deep and thoughtful questions that bring awareness to the underlying motivations, values, and potential consequences of a decision. We provide a framework for entrepreneurs to engage in reflective inquiry and gain clarity before making important decisions.

3. Non-attachment to Outcomes: Mindful decision making involves letting go of attachment to specific outcomes and embracing a sense of openness and curiosity. We explore the practice of non-attachment and how it can help entrepreneurs navigate uncertainty and make decisions with a flexible mindset.

4. Mindful Risk Assessment: Entrepreneurship often involves taking risks, and mindful decision making includes assessing risks with clarity and discernment. We discuss techniques for objectively evaluating risks, considering potential consequences, and managing fear and uncertainty.

Benefits of Mindful Decision Making:

Integrating mindfulness into the decision-making process offers numerous benefits for entrepreneurs. In this section, we explore the advantages of mindful decision making, including:

1. Enhanced Clarity and Focus: Mindfulness practices sharpen focus and reduce mental clutter, allowing entrepreneurs to make decisions with increased clarity and precision.

2. Improved Emotional Intelligence: Mindful decision making incorporates emotional intelligence, enabling entrepreneurs to consider the emotions and perspectives of others and make decisions that nurture positive relationships.

3. Increased Adaptability and Resilience: Mindful decision making fosters adaptability and resilience by embracing uncertainty and being open to new possibilities. Entrepreneurs can navigate challenges and pivot when needed, leading to greater long-term success.

4. Alignment with Purpose and Values: Mindful decision making helps entrepreneurs align their choices with their purpose and values, ensuring that their decisions are in harmony with their overarching vision and mission.

Real-Life Examples of Mindful Decision Making

To illustrate the power of mindful decision making, we share real-life examples of entrepreneurs who have leveraged mindfulness in their decision-making processes. These stories demonstrate how mindfulness can lead to innovative solutions, strategic insights, and ethical decision making.

Conclusion:

Chapter 5 emphasizes the importance of mindful decision making in the entrepreneurial journey. By cultivating presence, tapping into intuition, and embracing a balanced approach, entrepreneurs can make decisions that are aligned with their purpose, values, and long-term vision. Mindful decision making enhances clarity, fosters adaptability, and promotes ethical and values-based choices. In the next chapter, we delve into the significance of cultivating mindful relationships and the impact they have on entrepreneurial success.

Chapter 6: Cultivating Authentic Leadership

Introduction:

Leadership is a critical component of entrepreneurship, and authentic leadership has emerged as a powerful and effective leadership style. In this chapter, we explore the concept of authentic leadership and its significance in entrepreneurial success. We delve into the qualities and characteristics of authentic leaders, discuss strategies for cultivating authentic leadership, and highlight the impact of authentic leadership on individuals, teams, and organizations.

Understanding Authentic Leadership:

Authentic leadership is rooted in self-awareness, transparency, and a genuine connection with others. It is about leading from a place of authenticity, integrity, and congruence with one's values and beliefs. In this section, we explore the key elements of authentic leadership:

1. Self-Reflection and Self-Awareness: Authentic leaders engage in ongoing self-reflection and cultivate a deep understanding of their strengths, weaknesses, values, and purpose. They are aware of their emotions, motivations, and behaviors, allowing them to lead with authenticity and clarity.

2. Transparency and Vulnerability: Authentic leaders are transparent and open, sharing their thoughts, feelings, and challenges with others. They create an environment of trust and psychological safety, where team members feel comfortable expressing themselves and contributing to the collective vision.

3. Consistency and Integrity: Authentic leaders align their actions with their words, demonstrating integrity and consistency in their behavior. They uphold their values and ethical principles, fostering trust and respect within their teams and organizations.

4. Empathy and Emotional Intelligence: Authentic leaders possess high levels of empathy and emotional intelligence, enabling them to understand and connect with the emotions and experiences of others. They create a supportive and inclusive environment where individuals feel valued and heard.

Cultivating Authentic Leadership:

Authentic leadership is not innate but can be cultivated through intentional practices and continuous growth. In this section, we explore strategies for entrepreneurs to cultivate authentic leadership:

1. Developing Self-Awareness: Self-awareness is the foundation of authentic leadership. We discuss techniques and practices such as mindfulness, journaling, and seeking feedback to deepen self-awareness and gain insights into one's strengths, weaknesses, and values.

2. Clarifying Personal Values: Authentic leaders align their leadership style with their personal values. We guide entrepreneurs through exercises to identify their core values, prioritize them, and integrate them into their decision-making processes.

3. Practicing Authentic Communication: Authentic leaders communicate openly and honestly, fostering a culture of trust and transparency. We explore techniques for effective and authentic communication, including active listening, giving and receiving feedback, and encouraging open dialogue.

4. Leading with Empathy: Authentic leaders cultivate empathy by actively listening, seeking to understand others' perspectives, and acknowledging their emotions and experiences. We discuss strategies for developing empathy and incorporating it into leadership practices.

5. Embracing Vulnerability: Authentic leaders embrace vulnerability as a strength, not a weakness. We explore ways for entrepreneurs to step out of their comfort zones, share their authentic selves, and create an environment where vulnerability is encouraged and valued.

6. Encouraging Personal Growth and Development: Authentic leaders prioritize their own personal growth and development, continuously seeking opportunities for learning, reflection, and improvement. We discuss the importance of self-care, setting boundaries, and investing in personal and professional growth.

Impact of Authentic Leadership:

Authentic leadership has a profound impact on individuals, teams, and organizations. In this section, we explore the benefits and outcomes of authentic leadership:

1. Trust and Engagement: Authentic leaders inspire trust and create an environment where individuals feel valued and empowered. This leads to higher levels of employee engagement, commitment, and loyalty.

2. Collaboration and Innovation: Authentic leaders foster a culture of collaboration, encouraging diverse perspectives and creative thinking. This enables teams to innovate, problem-solve, and drive meaningful change.

3. Resilience and Adaptability: Authentic leaders cultivate resilience and adaptability within their teams, empowering individuals to navigate challenges and embrace change. This creates a culture of resilience, agility, and continuous improvement.

4. Positive Organizational Culture: Authentic leadership shapes the organizational culture, promoting values such as honesty, authenticity, and ethical behavior. This cultivates a positive work environment, attracting and retaining top talent.

5. Sustainable Success: Authentic leaders prioritize long-term success over short-term gains. By aligning their leadership with their values and purpose, they create sustainable and impactful ventures that make a difference in the world.

Real-Life Examples of Authentic Leadership:

To illustrate the power of authentic leadership, we share real-life examples of entrepreneurs who have embodied authentic leadership qualities and achieved remarkable success. These stories showcase the positive impact of authentic leadership on individuals, teams, and the overall success of their ventures.

Conclusion:

Chapter 6 highlights the significance of cultivating authentic leadership in the entrepreneurial journey. By embracing self-awareness, transparency, empathy, and integrity, entrepreneurs can lead with authenticity and positively influence individuals and organizations. Authentic leadership fosters trust, engagement, collaboration, and resilience, creating a foundation for sustainable success. In the next chapter, we delve into the importance of fostering a mindful and inclusive organizational culture to maximize entrepreneurial potential.

Chapter 7: Mindful Communication and Collaboration

Introduction:

Effective communication and collaboration are essential for entrepreneurial success. In this chapter, we explore the transformative power of mindful communication and collaboration in building strong relationships, fostering teamwork, and driving innovation. We delve into the principles of mindful communication, discuss strategies for cultivating a mindful communication style, and highlight the benefits of incorporating mindfulness into collaborative efforts.

Understanding Mindful Communication:

Mindful communication involves the conscious and intentional exchange of ideas, thoughts, and emotions, with a focus on deep listening, empathy, and clarity. It goes beyond surface-level conversations and seeks to foster genuine connection and understanding. In this section, we explore the core principles of mindful communication:

1. Presence and Active Listening: Mindful communication requires being fully present and engaged in the conversation. It involves active listening, where individuals attentively focus on the speaker, set aside distractions, and strive to understand the message being conveyed.

2. Empathy and Compassion: Mindful communication embraces empathy and compassion, recognizing and acknowledging the emotions and experiences of others. It involves putting oneself in the shoes of others, seeking to understand their perspectives, and responding with kindness and understanding.

3. Nonviolent Communication: Nonviolent communication, developed by Marshall Rosenberg, is a powerful framework for mindful communication. It focuses on expressing needs, listening with empathy, and fostering understanding and connection.

4. Clarity and Mindful Expression: Mindful communication emphasizes clear and intentional expression of thoughts and feelings. It involves choosing words carefully, being mindful of tone and body language, and ensuring that the message is conveyed in a way that promotes understanding and collaboration.

Cultivating Mindful Communication:

To cultivate mindful communication, entrepreneurs can adopt specific strategies and practices. In this section, we explore techniques for cultivating mindful communication:

1. Mindful Speaking: Mindful speaking involves pausing before speaking, choosing words mindfully, and expressing oneself with clarity and authenticity. We discuss techniques such as breath awareness, self-reflection, and practicing concise and effective communication.

2. Deep Listening: Deep listening is an essential aspect of mindful communication. We explore techniques for active listening, such as maintaining eye contact, giving full attention, and reflecting on what is being said. We also discuss the importance of suspending judgment and cultivating a non-reactive mindset.

3. Mindful Feedback and Conflict Resolution: Mindful communication includes providing feedback and resolving conflicts in a mindful and constructive manner. We provide strategies for giving and receiving feedback mindfully, as well as techniques for managing conflicts with empathy and respect.

4. Cultivating Emotional Intelligence: Mindful communication is closely intertwined with emotional intelligence. We explore practices for developing emotional intelligence, such as self-awareness, recognizing and managing emotions, and empathetic understanding of others' emotions.

Benefits of Mindful Communication and Collaboration:

Integrating mindfulness into communication and collaboration yields numerous benefits for entrepreneurs and their ventures. In this section, we explore the advantages of mindful communication and collaboration:

1. Enhanced Relationship Building: Mindful communication fosters authentic and meaningful connections, building trust and strengthening relationships. This creates a positive and supportive environment where individuals can thrive and collaborate effectively.

2. Improved Teamwork and Collaboration: Mindful communication facilitates effective teamwork and collaboration by promoting open and transparent communication, active listening, and understanding. This leads to increased productivity, creativity, and innovation within the team.

3. Conflict Resolution and Problem-Solving: Mindful communication provides a foundation for effective conflict resolution and problem-solving. By cultivating empathy, non-reactivity, and clarity, entrepreneurs can navigate conflicts with understanding and find constructive solutions.

4. Inclusive and Diverse Work Environment: Mindful communication embraces diversity and inclusion, valuing different perspectives and creating a safe space for all voices to be heard. This fosters a culture of innovation and fosters creativity and innovation.

5. Enhanced Customer Relationships: Mindful communication extends beyond internal collaboration and includes interactions with customers and stakeholders. By listening actively, understanding their needs, and responding with empathy, entrepreneurs can build strong and long-lasting customer relationships.

Real-Life Examples of Mindful Communication and Collaboration:

To illustrate the power of mindful communication and collaboration, we share real-life examples of entrepreneurs who have embraced mindful practices in their communication and collaborative efforts. These stories demonstrate the positive impact of mindful communication on team dynamics, innovation, and organizational success.

Conclusion:

Chapter 7 emphasizes the transformative nature of mindful communication and collaboration in the entrepreneurial journey. By practicing presence, empathy, and clarity in communication, entrepreneurs can build strong relationships, foster effective teamwork, and drive innovation. Mindful communication cultivates understanding, collaboration, and inclusivity, leading to enhanced creativity, productivity, and organizational success. In the next chapter, we delve into the significance of fostering a culture of well-being and resilience in entrepreneurial ventures.

Chapter 8: Creating a Mindful Work Environment

Introduction:

The work environment plays a crucial role in the success and well-being of entrepreneurs and their teams. In this chapter, we explore the importance of creating a mindful work environment and its impact on productivity, innovation, and employee satisfaction. We delve into the key elements of a mindful work environment, discuss strategies for cultivating mindfulness within the workplace, and highlight the benefits of fostering a culture of well-being and resilience.

Understanding a Mindful Work Environment:

A mindful work environment is one that promotes presence, awareness, and overall well-being. It prioritizes the mental, emotional, and physical health of individuals, and encourages a positive and inclusive culture. In this section, we explore the key elements of a mindful work environment:

1. Psychological Safety: A mindful work environment fosters psychological safety, where individuals feel comfortable expressing themselves, taking risks, and sharing their ideas without fear of judgment or retribution. This encourages open communication, collaboration, and innovation.

2. Work-Life Balance: A mindful work environment recognizes the importance of work-life balance and supports individuals in achieving it. It promotes healthy boundaries, encourages time for rest and rejuvenation, and values the well-being of employees beyond their work responsibilities.

3. Mindful Leadership: Mindful leaders set the tone for a mindful work environment. They lead by example, prioritize the well-being of their team members, and create an atmosphere of trust, respect, and support. Mindful leaders promote collaboration, open communication, and personal growth.

4. Mindful Practices and Rituals: A mindful work environment incorporates practices and rituals that cultivate mindfulness, such as meditation sessions, mindfulness workshops, and regular check-ins to promote self-awareness and stress management.

Cultivating a Mindful Work Environment:

Creating a mindful work environment requires intentional effort and a commitment to the well-being of employees. In this section, we explore strategies for cultivating a mindful work environment:

1. Cultivating Mindful Leadership: Mindful leadership sets the foundation for a mindful work environment. We discuss techniques and practices for leaders to develop self-awareness, emotional intelligence, and empathy, and to create a culture that values mindfulness and well-being.

2. Promoting Work-Life Integration: A mindful work environment acknowledges the importance of work-life integration and supports employees in achieving it. We explore strategies such as flexible work arrangements, encouraging breaks and vacations, and fostering a supportive culture that values personal well-being.

3. Nurturing Psychological Safety: Psychological safety is essential for a mindful work environment. We discuss techniques for fostering psychological safety, including creating an environment of trust, encouraging open communication, and providing opportunities for feedback and growth.

4. Incorporating Mindfulness Practices: Mindfulness practices can be integrated into the daily work routine to cultivate a mindful work environment. We explore techniques such as brief mindfulness exercises, mindful meetings, and incorporating moments of pause and reflection throughout the workday.

5. Encouraging Collaboration and Collective Growth: A mindful work environment promotes collaboration, teamwork, and collective growth. We discuss strategies for fostering a collaborative culture, such as promoting shared goals, encouraging diverse perspectives, and creating opportunities for skill-building and knowledge-sharing.

Benefits of a Mindful Work Environment:

Fostering a mindful work environment yields numerous benefits for entrepreneurs, employees, and the overall success of the organization. In this section, we explore the advantages of a mindful work environment:

1. Increased Productivity and Innovation: A mindful work environment enhances focus, creativity, and problem-solving abilities, leading to increased productivity and innovation within the organization.

2. Enhanced Employee Well-being and Satisfaction: A mindful work environment prioritizes employee well-being, leading to higher levels of job satisfaction, engagement, and retention. It reduces stress, burnout, and promotes a positive work-life balance.

3. Improved Collaboration and Team Dynamics: A mindful work environment fosters collaboration, trust, and effective communication among team members. This leads to improved teamwork, synergy, and collective success.

4. Resilience and Adaptability: A mindful work environment cultivates resilience and adaptability within individuals and teams. It provides the tools and support needed to navigate challenges, embrace change, and bounce back from setbacks.

Real-Life Examples of Mindful Work Environments:

To illustrate the impact of a mindful work environment, we share real-life examples of organizations that have successfully created a culture of mindfulness and well-being. These examples highlight the positive outcomes, including increased employee satisfaction, improved productivity, and organizational success.

Conclusion:

Chapter 8 emphasizes the importance of creating a mindful work environment in the entrepreneurial journey. By prioritizing employee well-being, promoting mindfulness practices, and fostering a culture of collaboration and resilience, entrepreneurs can create a space where individuals thrive, creativity flourishes, and success is sustainable. A mindful work environment enhances productivity, innovation, and employee satisfaction, contributing to the overall success of the organization. In the next chapter, we explore the role of mindful growth and continuous learning in entrepreneurial endeavors.

Part III: Mindfulness in Action: Real-Life Entrepreneurial Stories

Introduction:

In Part III, we delve into real-life entrepreneurial stories that showcase the application of mindfulness in action. These stories provide inspiration and practical insights into how mindfulness can be integrated into various aspects of entrepreneurship. From navigating challenges to fostering creativity and making ethical decisions, these stories demonstrate the power of mindfulness in shaping successful entrepreneurial journeys.

Conclusion:

Part III presents real-life entrepreneurial stories that demonstrate the application of mindfulness in various aspects of entrepreneurship. These stories illustrate how mindfulness can contribute to startup success, foster innovation and creativity, and guide ethical leadership. By showcasing the experiences of these entrepreneurs, we aim to inspire readers to integrate mindfulness into their own entrepreneurial journeys and unleash their full potential.

Chapter 9: Mindful Entrepreneurs' Success Stories

Introduction:

In Chapter 9, we dive into the captivating stories of successful entrepreneurs who attribute their achievements to the practice of mindfulness. These individuals have embraced mindfulness as a guiding principle in their entrepreneurial journeys, allowing them to navigate challenges, find clarity, and cultivate success. Through their inspiring experiences, we gain valuable insights into how mindfulness can shape entrepreneurial paths and contribute to long-lasting accomplishments.

1. Sarah Thompson - Harnessing Focus and Clarity

Sarah Thompson, the founder of a thriving e-commerce company, credits mindfulness for her ability to harness focus and clarity in the fast-paced entrepreneurial world. Facing the overwhelming demands of managing a growing business, Sarah turned to mindfulness to bring calm and centeredness into her daily life. By incorporating mindfulness practices such as meditation and mindful breathing, she developed the capacity to prioritize tasks effectively, make strategic decisions, and maintain a healthy work-life balance. Through the power of mindfulness, Sarah transformed her approach to entrepreneurship, resulting in increased productivity, improved decision-making, and sustained business growth.

2. David Patel - Embracing Resilience and Adaptability

David Patel, an entrepreneur in the technology industry, shares his journey of embracing mindfulness as a tool for resilience and adaptability. As an ambitious entrepreneur, David encountered numerous obstacles and uncertainties along his path. Through the practice of mindfulness, including meditation and self-reflection, he cultivated the ability to stay present and grounded, even in the face of adversity. By embracing the present moment and adopting a mindset of acceptance, David developed the resilience necessary to bounce back from failures, adapt to changing circumstances, and lead his team through challenging times. His story exemplifies the transformative power of mindfulness in building resilience and fostering a growth mindset.

3. Lisa Chen - Cultivating Emotional Intelligence and Authentic Leadership

Lisa Chen, the founder of a successful social enterprise, attributes her accomplishments to the cultivation of emotional intelligence and authentic leadership through mindfulness. Recognizing the significance of fostering deep connections with her team, Lisa integrated mindfulness practices into her leadership style. By developing self-awareness and empathy through mindfulness, she created a work environment where her team members felt seen, heard, and valued. This led to enhanced collaboration, increased employee satisfaction, and a positive organizational culture. Lisa's story illustrates how mindfulness can facilitate authentic leadership, nurture emotional intelligence, and create a thriving entrepreneurial ecosystem.

4. Mark Johnson - Unleashing Creativity and Driving Innovation

Mark Johnson, a serial entrepreneur and creative visionary, shares how mindfulness has been instrumental in unleashing his creativity and driving innovation. Through mindfulness practices such as mindfulness walks and creative visualization, Mark taps into his inner creativity and intuition, enabling him to generate groundbreaking ideas and develop innovative solutions. By cultivating a state of open awareness and letting go of mental barriers, Mark has been able to pioneer new products and services, setting his ventures apart from the competition. His story highlights the transformative power of mindfulness in unlocking one's creative potential and fostering entrepreneurial innovation.

Conclusion:

Chapter 9 showcases the captivating stories of mindful entrepreneurs who have achieved remarkable success by integrating mindfulness into their entrepreneurial journeys. These individuals serve as inspiring examples of how mindfulness can enhance focus, resilience, emotional intelligence, and creativity, resulting in business growth, authentic leadership, and innovative solutions. Their experiences remind us that mindfulness is not merely a personal practice but a powerful tool for entrepreneurial success. By embracing mindfulness, entrepreneurs can cultivate the inner resources needed to navigate challenges, make wise decisions, and thrive in their ventures. In the next chapter, we delve into the role of mindfulness in ethical decision-making and social impact entrepreneurship.

Lessons Learned and Key Takeaways

Throughout "The Mindful Entrepreneur: Cultivating Success with Presence and Purpose," we have explored the profound impact of mindfulness on entrepreneurial journeys. As we conclude our journey, it is important to reflect on the key lessons learned and takeaways from this exploration.

1. Mindfulness is a Powerful Tool: Mindfulness is not just a passing trend; it is a powerful tool that can profoundly transform the entrepreneurial experience. By cultivating a present-moment awareness, entrepreneurs can enhance focus, decision-making, resilience, and creativity.

2. Presence is Key: The power of presence cannot be overstated. Being fully present in each moment allows entrepreneurs to embrace challenges, seize opportunities, and make conscious choices. Mindfulness enables entrepreneurs to bring their full attention and energy to their work, resulting in more meaningful and impactful outcomes.

3. Purpose Drives Success: Aligning with a clear sense of purpose is vital for entrepreneurial success. When entrepreneurs have a deep understanding of their values, vision, and mission, they are better equipped to make strategic decisions, stay motivated during tough times, and create a lasting impact.

4. Resilience is Nurtured: Mindfulness practices foster resilience by helping entrepreneurs navigate the inevitable ups and downs of the entrepreneurial journey. By cultivating mindfulness, entrepreneurs can develop the ability to bounce back from setbacks, adapt to change, and maintain a positive mindset in the face of challenges.

5. Authentic Leadership Matters: Mindfulness and authentic leadership go hand in hand. Mindful entrepreneurs lead with empathy, self-awareness, and a genuine concern for the well-being of their team members. This creates a supportive work environment, fosters collaboration, and enhances overall team performance.

6. Collaboration Fuels Innovation: Mindfulness promotes collaboration and collective growth. By encouraging diverse perspectives, open communication, and shared goals, entrepreneurs can tap into the collective wisdom of their teams and drive innovative solutions.

7. Well-being is Essential: Prioritizing well-being is not a luxury but a necessity for sustainable success. Mindful entrepreneurs recognize the importance of work-life balance, self-care, and maintaining a healthy mental and physical state. By nurturing their well-being, entrepreneurs can sustain their energy, creativity, and passion for their work.

8. Ethical Decision-Making Matters: Mindfulness plays a crucial role in ethical decision-making. Mindful entrepreneurs approach ethical dilemmas with compassion, integrity, and a deep understanding of the potential impact of their choices. By making ethically sound decisions, entrepreneurs build trust, foster positive relationships, and create businesses with long-term sustainability.

9. Continuous Learning and Growth: Mindful entrepreneurs embrace a mindset of continuous learning and growth. They understand that their journey is a constant evolution, and they seek opportunities to expand their knowledge, skills, and perspectives. By cultivating a growth mindset, entrepreneurs can adapt to changing environments, seize new opportunities, and stay ahead in a rapidly evolving business landscape.

10. Mindfulness is for Everyone: Mindfulness is not exclusive to a select few; it is accessible and beneficial for all entrepreneurs. Regardless of background, experience, or industry, anyone can incorporate mindfulness practices into their entrepreneurial journey and experience the transformative benefits.

In conclusion, "The Mindful Entrepreneur: Cultivating Success with Presence and Purpose" has explored the immense potential of mindfulness in entrepreneurial endeavors. From harnessing focus and resilience to fostering authentic leadership and driving innovation, mindfulness is a foundational element for success. By incorporating mindfulness into their lives and businesses, entrepreneurs can cultivate presence, purpose, and well-being, leading to sustainable success and fulfillment in their entrepreneurial journeys.

Chapter 10: Mindfulness in the Future of Entrepreneurship

Introduction:

As we look toward the future of entrepreneurship, it is clear that mindfulness will continue to play a vital role in shaping the landscape. In Chapter 10, we explore how mindfulness is poised to transform the way we approach business, innovation, and leadership. From emerging trends to technological advancements, we examine how mindfulness can guide entrepreneurs in navigating the evolving entrepreneurial landscape and driving sustainable success.

1. The Rise of Conscious Capitalism:

In recent years, there has been a growing movement toward conscious capitalism, where businesses prioritize social and environmental impact alongside financial success. Mindful entrepreneurs are at the forefront of this movement, recognizing the importance of integrating purpose, ethics, and sustainability into their ventures. By aligning their businesses with a higher purpose and incorporating mindfulness practices, entrepreneurs can create organizations that have a positive impact on society and the planet.

2. Mindful Innovation and Technology:

As technology continues to advance at an unprecedented pace, entrepreneurs need to find ways to harness its power mindfully. Mindful innovation involves leveraging technology while staying connected to our humanity. By using mindfulness practices, entrepreneurs can cultivate the awareness and discernment necessary to make ethical decisions regarding the use of technology, ensuring it serves humanity's greater good.

3. Mindfulness in Remote Work and Virtual Collaboration:

The COVID-19 pandemic has accelerated the adoption of remote work and virtual collaboration. As these practices become more prevalent, entrepreneurs must explore how to cultivate mindfulness in this new work environment. Mindfulness can support remote workers in managing distractions, maintaining work-life balance, and fostering effective communication and collaboration. By incorporating mindfulness into virtual work practices, entrepreneurs can create a harmonious and productive remote work culture.

4. Mindful Leadership in a Diverse World:

Diversity and inclusion have become critical considerations for entrepreneurial success. Mindful leadership recognizes the value of diverse perspectives and seeks to create an inclusive and equitable work environment. By practicing mindfulness, entrepreneurs can develop the awareness, empathy, and compassion needed to lead diverse teams effectively and foster an inclusive culture where everyone feels valued and heard.

5. Mindfulness and Well-being in the Gig Economy:

The gig economy is rapidly expanding, with more individuals pursuing freelance and independent work. In this context, the well-being of entrepreneurs and independent workers becomes paramount. Mindfulness practices can help entrepreneurs in the gig economy manage the challenges of uncertainty, isolation, and work-life integration. By incorporating mindfulness into their routines, entrepreneurs can cultivate self-care, resilience, and a healthy work-life balance.

6. Mindfulness and Artificial Intelligence:

The integration of artificial intelligence (AI) into various aspects of business presents both opportunities and challenges. Mindful entrepreneurs recognize the need to approach AI mindfully, considering its ethical implications and potential impact on society. By cultivating mindfulness, entrepreneurs can make informed decisions regarding the use of AI, ensuring that it aligns with their values and contributes to the betterment of humanity.

7. Mindfulness and Sustainable Business Practices:

In an era of growing environmental concerns, sustainable business practices are no longer optional but essential. Mindful entrepreneurs embrace sustainability as a core value, implementing environmentally friendly practices and mindful resource management. By integrating mindfulness into their decision-making processes, entrepreneurs can identify innovative solutions that prioritize sustainability and contribute to a regenerative economy.

Conclusion:

Chapter 10 explores the future of entrepreneurship through the lens of mindfulness. As the entrepreneurial landscape continues to evolve, mindfulness will serve as a guiding force, enabling entrepreneurs to navigate emerging trends, harness technology mindfully, lead diverse teams, prioritize well-being, and cultivate sustainable practices. By embracing mindfulness in their entrepreneurial endeavors, individuals can not only achieve success but also create businesses that have a positive impact on society and the planet. As we embark on this exciting future, mindfulness will remain an essential tool for entrepreneurial success, empowering entrepreneurs to thrive amidst complexity, uncertainty, and rapid change.

Conclusion: Cultivating Success with Presence and Purpose

Throughout the pages of "The Mindful Entrepreneur: Cultivating Success with Presence and Purpose," we have embarked on a transformative journey into the world of mindfulness and entrepreneurship. We have explored the profound impact of mindfulness on the entrepreneurial mindset, decision-making, leadership, communication, and the overall success of ventures. As we conclude this enlightening exploration, it is essential to reflect on the key insights and lessons learned, and reinforce the significance of cultivating presence and purpose in the entrepreneurial journey.

1. The Power of Presence:

Presence is a foundational element of entrepreneurial success. Being fully present in each moment allows entrepreneurs to immerse themselves in their work, connect deeply with others, and seize opportunities with clarity and intention. Mindfulness practices, such as meditation, breath awareness, and body scans, serve as gateways to the present moment, helping entrepreneurs cultivate focus, concentration, and a heightened sense of awareness. By embracing the power of presence, entrepreneurs can break free from the distractions of the past and future, enabling them to make informed decisions, tap into their intuition, and unlock their full creative potential.

2. The Importance of Purpose:

Aligning with a clear sense of purpose is vital for sustained success and fulfillment in entrepreneurship. Purpose provides entrepreneurs with a compass, guiding their decisions, actions, and the overall direction of their ventures. It serves as a driving force that propels entrepreneurs forward during challenging times, fuels their passion and motivation, and fosters a sense of meaning and fulfillment in their work. Mindful entrepreneurs actively seek to uncover their authentic purpose by reflecting on their values, strengths, and the impact they aspire to create in the world. By anchoring themselves in purpose, entrepreneurs can navigate the complexities of the entrepreneurial journey with clarity, resilience, and a deep sense of fulfillment.

3. Mindfulness as a Catalyst for Success:

Mindfulness serves as a catalyst for success in entrepreneurship by enhancing key entrepreneurial attributes and skills. By cultivating mindfulness, entrepreneurs develop the ability to manage stress and uncertainty effectively, navigate challenges with resilience, and maintain a balanced perspective amidst the highs and lows of the entrepreneurial journey. Mindfulness also fosters self-awareness, allowing entrepreneurs to recognize and harness their strengths, as well as identify and address areas for growth. Furthermore, mindfulness cultivates empathy and compassion, enabling entrepreneurs to build strong relationships, lead authentically, and create thriving organizational cultures. By integrating mindfulness practices into their daily lives, entrepreneurs can unlock their full potential and pave the way for long-lasting success.

4. The Mindful Decision-Making Advantage:

Mindfulness plays a pivotal role in decision-making, offering entrepreneurs a competitive advantage in a fast-paced and complex business environment. By practicing mindfulness, entrepreneurs develop the ability to step back, observe their thoughts and emotions, and approach decisions from a place of clarity and objectivity. Mindful decision-making involves gathering information, considering multiple perspectives, and carefully evaluating the potential consequences of each choice. It also entails listening to one's intuition and being attuned to subtle signals and insights that arise in the present moment. By integrating mindfulness into the decision-making process, entrepreneurs can make wise, values-driven choices that align with their vision, purpose, and long-term goals.

5. Authentic Leadership through Mindfulness:

Mindfulness is a catalyst for authentic leadership, enabling entrepreneurs to lead with integrity, empathy, and purpose. By cultivating self-awareness, mindful entrepreneurs develop a deep understanding of their strengths, weaknesses, and values, allowing them to lead from a place of authenticity. Mindful leaders actively listen to their team members, create a safe and inclusive environment, and foster collaboration and open communication. They prioritize the well-being and growth of their employees, recognizing that a supportive and engaged workforce is essential for long-term success. Mindful leadership not only inspires trust and loyalty but also creates an organizational culture that thrives on creativity, innovation, and collective success.

6. Mindful Communication as a Catalyst for Collaboration:

Effective communication is the lifeblood of successful entrepreneurship. Mindful entrepreneurs understand the power of clear, compassionate, and attentive communication in building strong relationships, fostering collaboration, and driving meaningful outcomes. Mindful communication involves active listening, non-judgmental presence, and genuine curiosity. It requires the ability to express oneself authentically and empathetically, while also being receptive to diverse perspectives and feedback. By integrating mindful communication practices, entrepreneurs can break down barriers, cultivate trust and respect, and create a collaborative work environment where ideas flourish and innovation thrives.

7. Creating a Mindful Work Environment:

Entrepreneurs have the power to shape the work environment and culture within their ventures. By infusing mindfulness into the organizational fabric, entrepreneurs can create a work environment that nurtures well-being, fosters creativity, and supports sustainable success. Mindful entrepreneurs prioritize work-life balance, encourage self-care practices, and provide opportunities for personal and professional growth. They design physical spaces that promote relaxation, focus, and creativity. Mindful work environments embrace diversity, equity, and inclusion, recognizing the unique strengths and contributions of each individual. By creating a mindful work environment, entrepreneurs empower their team members, enhance productivity, and attract and retain top talent.

In conclusion, "The Mindful Entrepreneur: Cultivating Success with Presence and Purpose" has explored the profound impact of mindfulness on entrepreneurship. By embracing mindfulness, entrepreneurs can develop a deeper connection with themselves, their ventures, and the world around them. Mindfulness cultivates presence, purpose, and resilience, enabling entrepreneurs to navigate challenges, make informed decisions, lead with authenticity, foster collaboration, and create a work environment that supports well-being and innovation. As entrepreneurs embark on their journeys, the integration of mindfulness into their lives and ventures will pave the way for sustainable success, personal fulfillment, and a positive impact on society. May this book inspire and guide aspiring and seasoned entrepreneurs alike to cultivate success with presence and purpose.

Appendix: Mindfulness Practices and Resources

In "The Mindful Entrepreneur: Cultivating Success with Presence and Purpose," we have explored the transformative potential of mindfulness in the entrepreneurial journey. As you embark on your own mindfulness practice, this appendix provides a collection of mindfulness exercises and resources to support your ongoing development and integration of mindfulness into your entrepreneurial endeavors.

Mindfulness Practices:

1. Mindful Breathing: Take a few moments each day to focus on your breath. Close your eyes, bring your attention to your breath, and observe the sensation of each inhale and exhale. This simple practice helps anchor you in the present moment and cultivates a sense of calm and clarity.

2. Body Scan Meditation: Set aside time to scan your body from head to toe, paying attention to any sensations or areas of tension. Bring a gentle awareness to each part of your body, relaxing and releasing any tension you may find along the way.

3. Mindful Walking: Engage in mindful walking by paying close attention to the physical sensations of each step. Feel the ground beneath your feet, notice the rhythm of your stride, and observe the sights, sounds, and smells around you as you walk.

4. Loving-Kindness Meditation: Practice cultivating loving-kindness by extending well-wishes and compassion to yourself and others. Begin by offering loving-kindness to yourself, then gradually expand your focus to include loved ones, colleagues, and even those you find challenging.

5. Mindful Eating: Slow down and bring awareness to the experience of eating. Notice the flavors, textures, and sensations of each bite. Pay attention to the nourishment that food provides and savor each moment.

6. Mindful Work Breaks: Take short mindful breaks throughout the day to pause, breathe, and reset. Use these moments to bring your attention back to the present, release tension, and re-energize.

7. Gratitude Practice: Cultivate gratitude by reflecting on the things you are grateful for in your entrepreneurial journey. Take a few moments each day to write down or mentally acknowledge the blessings and opportunities that come your way.

Mindfulness Resources:

1. Meditation Apps: Explore popular meditation apps such as Headspace, Calm, and Insight Timer, which offer guided meditations, mindfulness exercises, and resources to support your practice.

2. Mindfulness Courses and Workshops: Consider enrolling in mindfulness courses or workshops that provide in-depth teachings and guidance on integrating mindfulness into your entrepreneurial life. Look for local offerings or online platforms that offer mindfulness programs.

3. Mindfulness Books: Dive deeper into mindfulness with books such as "The Miracle of Mindfulness" by Thich Nhat Hanh, "Full Catastrophe Living" by Jon Kabat-Zinn, or "Mindfulness: A Practical Guide to Finding Peace in a Frantic World" by Mark Williams and Danny Penman.

4. Mindfulness Retreats: Attend mindfulness retreats or workshops led by experienced teachers and practitioners. These immersive experiences provide a supportive environment for deepening your mindfulness practice and connecting with like-minded individuals.

5. Online Communities and Forums: Join online communities and forums focused on mindfulness and entrepreneurship. Engage with others who share your interests, exchange ideas, and seek support and guidance.

Remember, mindfulness is a journey that requires patience, consistency, and self-compassion. As an entrepreneur, integrating mindfulness into your daily life can have a profound impact on your well-being, decision-making, and overall success. Explore these practices and resources, and adapt them to suit your unique needs and preferences. May your mindfulness journey bring you clarity, purpose, and a deep sense of fulfillment as you cultivate success with presence and purpose.

Note: The practices and resources provided in this appendix are for informational purposes only. Please consult with a qualified mindfulness teacher or healthcare professional if you have any specific concerns or conditions related to mindfulness practice.